DASTARDLY DELIGHTFUL
MONSTERS

DASTARDLY DELIGHTFUL
MONSTERS

Create your own monsters to unleash mayhem

PaRragon

Bath · New York · Singapore · Hong Kong · Cologne · Delhi
Melbourne · Amsterdam · Johannesburg · Auckland · Shenzhen

MONSTER MAYHEM!

First published by Parragon in 2012

Parragon
Queen Street House
4 Queen Street
Bath BA1 1HE, UK
www.parragon.com

Copyright © Parragon Books Ltd 2012
Designed by Pink Creative
Illustrations by Caroline Martin
Project managed by Frances Prior-Reeves

ISBN 978-1-4454-8863-9

Printed in China

 CUSHION MONSTER 8

 DIZZY DIE 12

 GUTSY 16

 SOCK MONSTER 20

 WEBSTER THE WEBCAM MONSTER 24

 PLAY IT LOUD! 28

 MANIC MOUSE 32

 FULL OF BEANS 36

MONSTER TEMPLATES 40

INDEX 48

DASTARDLY DELIGHTFUL
MONSTERS

Monsters are all around us but only a few, with a keen eye, can see them in hiding. They're not just hidden under your bed any more; they've become much more cunning. The key to dealing with monsters is knowing their weaknesses. Do you need music to make them fall asleep or water to drench the horror out of them? Make sure you know before you create your own little critters.

Liven up your life with a little monster creation! Become the Frankenstein of your own house as you get to grips with making these fun and scary characters. All you need to create each monster is listed at the start of the instructions. For all projects you'll need a pair of scissors and a needle. You might also find pins helpful to attach your paper template to the fabric before cutting. All the templates you need are included in the back, ready for you to copy them, cut them out and start creating your own monsters.

If you want to start with an easier project try Webster (p.24) and move on to the complex monster intricacies of Dizzy Die (p.12). They all seem sweet at first, but turn your back and they'll be running riot and causing havoc every which way. You have been warned!

MAKING `CUSHION MONSTER`

1 Photocopy or trace all the templates on page 40. Cut the two FRONT panels out of the blue fur. Cut the zip so it is the same length as the width of the FRONT panels.

2 Place one of the FRONT panels so the longest edge butts up against one edge of the zip. The fur side should be face up, with the zip face down. Sew the FRONT panel to the zip with white thread.

3 Now sew the other FRONT panel to the zip in the same way.

MATERIALS

Blue fur, patterned fabric, red felt, peach felt, white felt

White embroidery thread

1 zip 14cm (5½ inches) long

Two buttons (one large, one smaller)

Toy stuffing

Pins, Craft glue

Embroidery needle

Scissors

Templates from page 40

CUSHION MONSTER

Don't make the mistake of sitting on this monster. You'll be afraid to sit down ever again and with those teeth, who could blame you?

4 Cut the two MOUTH parts from red felt. Now place one of the MOUTH parts so the long edge matches up to the zip edge. Make sure the MOUTH part is lying over the zip. Now stitch the MOUTH to the zip with white thread.

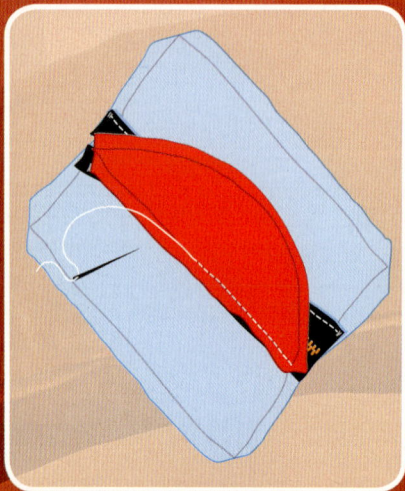

5 Repeat step 4, sewing the other side of the zip to the other half of the MOUTH.

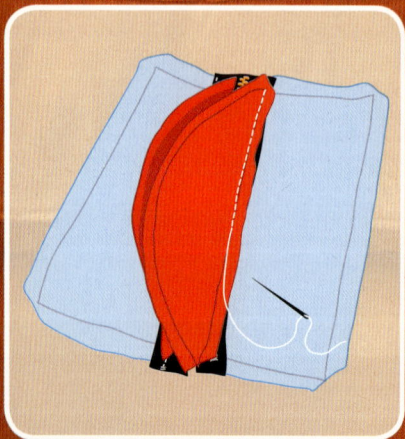

6 Now sew the two halves of the MOUTH together using white thread. Don't sew along the long straight edge nearest the zip as this is the opening of the mouth when the zip is open.

7 Cut out the BACK panel from the patterned fabric. Place the FRONT panels on a flat surface with the fur side face up and then place the BACK panel on top of this with the patterned side face down. Sew around three and ¾ sides only, to create a sort of pocket. You may find it a help to pin the fabrics together. Also, make sure that you close up the gap at the ends of the zip as well as possible.

8 Turn the cushion inside out and fill it with stuffing. Sew up the opening.

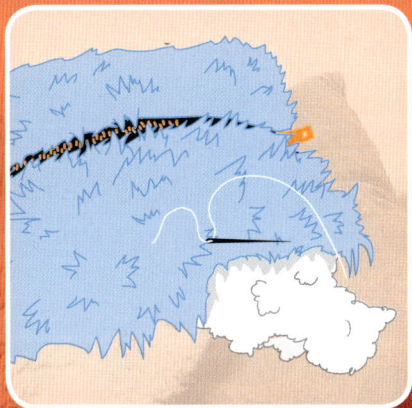

ARE YOU
SITTING
COMFORTABLY?

9 Sew the two buttons to the cushion using the white thread.

10 Cut out the two FINGER pieces from peach felt and the BONE and NAIL from white felt. Glue the BONE to one side of the FINGER.

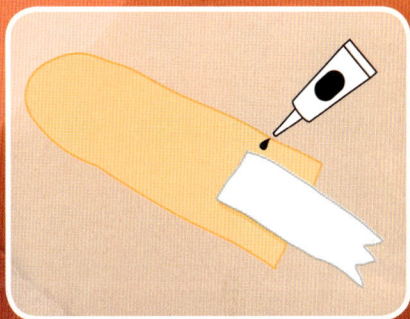

11 Glue the other FINGER piece to sandwich the BONE. Then glue the NAIL in place. Leave to dry and then the finger is ready for Cushion Monster to eat!

DIZZY DIE

Dizzy Die might not bring you the best of luck, especially if you blow on him. He'll probably take off a finger, rather than roll you a six, if you do that.

MATERIALS

Magenta felt, bright green felt,
white felt, black felt

Bright green and light blue
embroidery thread

Toy stuffing

1 small button

2 small blue beads

Pins, Craft glue, Iron

Embroidery needle, Scissors

Templates from page 41

MAKING `DIZZY DIE`

1 Photocopy or trace all the templates on page 41. Cut the four SIDE and two INSIDE panels from the magenta felt. Sew one SIDE panel to one INSIDE panel using the green thread.

2 Sew a second SIDE panel to the open side but leave one edge open. Now fill this with stuffing – just enough to keep the shape. If you overstuff it, the sides will start to bulge. Then close up the opening. Repeat, with the other INSIDE panel and two SIDE panels.

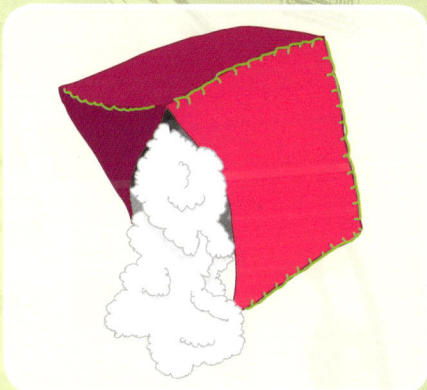

3 Stitch the two halves together using green thread, along one edge only so they hinge and come together to form a cube.

4 Cut out the BODY and use an iron, set to warm, to create the creases marked with the dotted lines. Be careful and don't burn your fingers!

5 Sew the BODY to the inside of the die using green thread.

6 Sew the button to the die, in the position shown, using green thread.

7 On the adjoining side and using six-strand green thread, sew a loop that will go over the button to hold the two halves of the die together. Don't make the loop too small or it will become impossible to undo it from the button.

8 Create the hair by sewing lengths of light blue, six-strand thread. Once there is a good amount of hair, separate the strands to make a 'messed-up' look.

10 Stitch a mouth using blue thread and glue on the TOOTH.

IN A SPIN!

9 Cut out both EYE pieces and sew a bead to each one using blue thread. Glue the EYES in place, making sure they are off centre so he looks dizzy.

11 Cut six magenta DOTS and glue them to the arms of the monster. Now carefully fold up the monster and close up the die and fasten in place.

12 Cut 21 black DOTS and glue them to each face of the die. Remember that opposite sides of a die always add up to seven. You will need to cut a couple of the DOTS in half as they will go over the opening on the sides of the die.

MATERIALS

Green felt, light blue felt,
white felt, red felt

Patterned fabric

1 zip 12cm (4½ inches)

2 small black buttons

Blue, pink and brown embroidery
thread

Toy stuffing

Pins

Embroidery needle

Scissors

Templates from page 42

MAKING `GUTSY`

1 Photocopy or trace all the templates on page 42. Cut the FRONT panel from the green felt. Stitch the zip to the back of the FRONT panel using the blue thread.

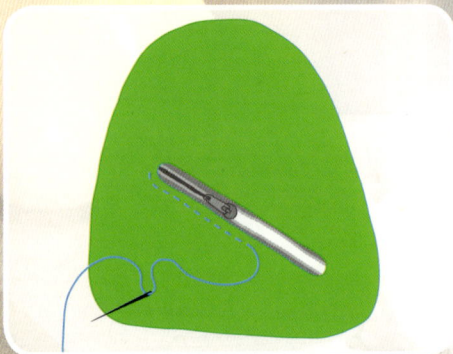

2 Cut the BACK panel from the patterned fabric and place it on the table with the print side face up. Cut the HANDS and FEET from the light blue felt and place them in position facing inwards. Place the FRONT panel on top of everything, face down. Make sure the zip is open. Now stitch around the edge with green thread. You may find it easier to pin the fabric first. Once done, turn Gutsy right side out through the zip.

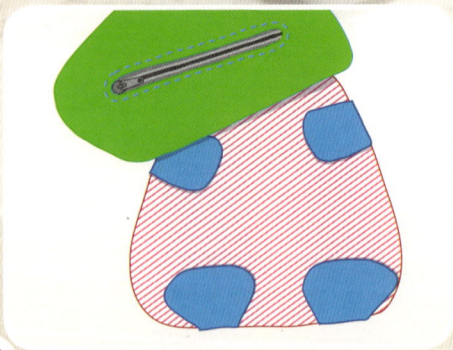

GUTSY

This monster is incredibly friendly, so much so he'll want to know you inside and out ... he's happy to show you his guts and just may not understand why he can't see yours.

3 Stitch Gutsy's mouth using six-strand brown thread.

4 Cut the two EYES from white felt. Stitch a button on each of the two EYES using black thread. Then glue the EYES to the FRONT.

5 Cut the six sections for the GUTS from red felt. Now sew the GUTS 1 panels together, then the GUTS 2 and then the GUTS 3, leaving the ends open.

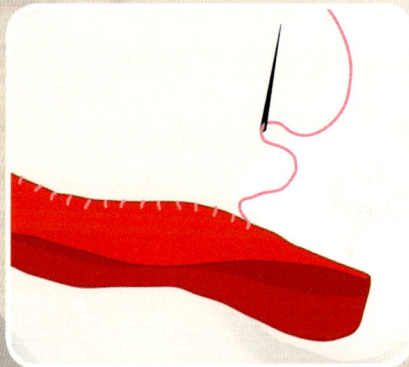

SEW AND STUFF

6 Now stuff each section of the GUTS with a small amount of stuffing. It's OK if the stuffing is a bit lumpy, guts are like that!

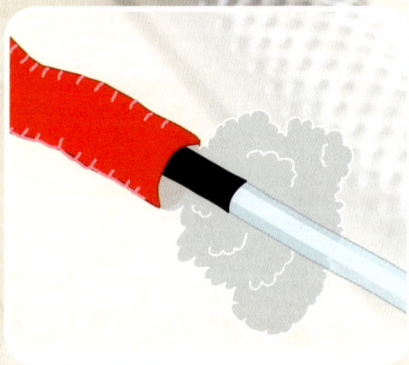

7 Join each of the three GUTS sections together with pink thread, making sure that GUTS 1 is at one end and GUTS 3 is at the other.

8 Sew the straight end of the GUTS to the seam on the inside of Gutsy. Scrunch up his guts and then stuff them in the body.

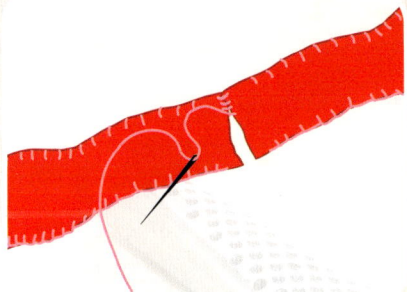

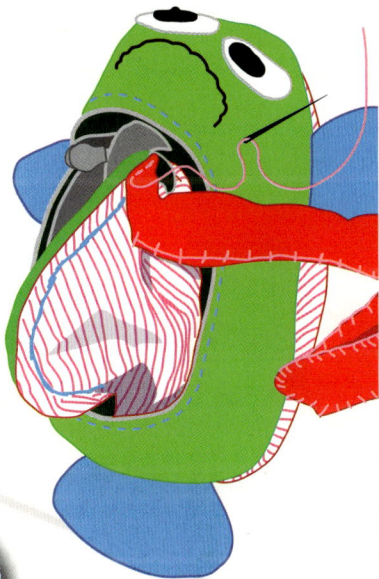

KNOW HIM
INSIDE
AND OUT

SOCK MONSTER

This monster loves freshly laundered socks and is often found skulking about your drawers when no one's looking. Now you know where all those socks go!

MATERIALS

White felt, black felt, green fur

Green and white embroidery thread

1 small and 1 medium button

Toy stuffing

Pins

Embroidery needle

Scissors

Templates from page 43

MAKING `SOCK MONSTER`

1 Photocopy or trace all the templates on page 43. Cut out the two MOUTH pieces from the black felt. Using the white thread, sew just the three sides of the square end together to create a sort of pocket.

2 Cut the FRONT PANEL from the green fur. Don't forget to also cut out the hole. Sew the MOUTH to the back of the FRONT PANEL with white thread.

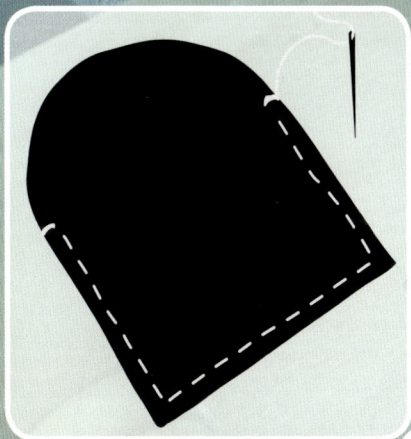

3 Turn the FRONT PANEL over so the fur is facing up. Cut the TEETH from white felt. Now sew the TEETH in position with just a couple of stitches using white thread.

5 Cut both EYE pieces from white felt. Place them in position and sew the two buttons, through each EYE and into the FRONT PANEL with white thread.

4 Cut the DOOR from white felt and stitch around the mouth with white thread.

6 Cut out the BACK PANEL, the two SIDE PANELS and the two END PANELS from white felt. First sew the SIDE PANELS and then the END PANELS to the BACK PANEL, then sew the SIDE PANELS and END PANELS together to create an open top box. Turn the box inside out.

7 Now sew the FRONT PANEL to the SIDE and END PANELS with white thread. Leave one end open.

9 Cut the SOCKS from white felt (or any colour that your monster prefers!) and sew the detail using white thread.

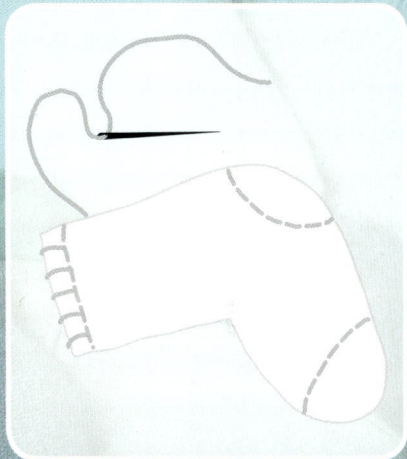

8 Finish the Sock Monster by filling him with stuffing. Make sure the inside of the mouth is sitting in the middle of the cavity with even amounts of stuffing either side. Sew up the last side.

GRRR!

Light green felt, white felt, dark green felt, red felt, brown felt

Brown and yellow embroidery thread

Green pipe cleaner

Toy stuffing

Pins

Craft glue

Embroidery needle

Scissors

Templates from page 44

MAKING `WEBSTER`

1 Photocopy or trace all the templates on page 44. Cut the two BODY pieces from light green felt. Cut the hole in the centre to the size of your webcam. On one of the BODY pieces, stitch the mouth using brown thread.

2 Cut the TOOTH pieces from white felt and glue them in position across the top of the mouth.

WEBSTER THE WEBCAM MONSTER

Once Webster has got himself wrapped around your webcam, you might be wise not to look him in the eye in case you change into something.

3 Now cut the two ARMS from dark green felt. Take the remaining BODY piece and place it face down. Place the two ARMS in position and hold them in place with a dab of glue.

4 Place the front of the BODY on top to sandwich the arms in place. Now stitch together around the outside using yellow thread, leaving the top edge open. Then stitch around the eye area.

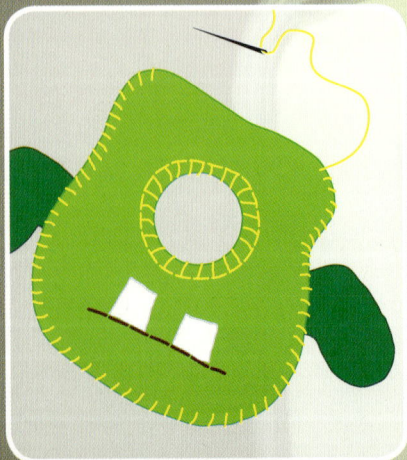

5 Stuff the BODY with a small amount of stuffing, just enough to give it some shape. You may find it easier to use a ballpoint pen to help push the stuffing to the bottom of the body cavity. Then stitch up the top edge to close up the body.

6 Cut the HORNS from red felt and the two sets of PAWS & CLAWS and the EYELASHES from brown felt. Glue them all in position.

GET CONNECTED

7 Turn Webster over. Using yellow thread, sew the pipe cleaner to half way between the eye and the bottom of the body.

8 Attach Webster to your webcam by wrapping the pipe cleaner around the back of the camera.

PLAY IT LOUD!

Not even hoodies are safe from the sonic boom of this crazed monster. Get your ear defenders ready, then plug him in.

MATERIALS

Light green felt, black felt, light blue felt, red felt, grey felt, white felt

Patterned fabric

1 large and 1 small button

Red, grey, light blue, light green, black and white embroidery thread

Toy stuffing

Pins, Craft glue

Embroidery needle

Scissors

Templates from page 45

MAKING `PLAY IT LOUD!`

1 Photocopy or trace all the templates on page 45. Cut the FACE and BACK PANEL from the light green felt, the MOUTH from black felt and the TEETH from white felt.

2 Lightly glue the TEETH to the MOUTH and then the MOUTH to the FACE PANEL. Now stitch around the edge of the felt with white thread.

3 Cut the EYE PANEL from the black felt. Using white thread, sew the two buttons to the EYE PANEL, then glue the EYE PANEL to the FACE PANEL, just above the mouth.

4 Cut the END BODY PANELS from red felt, the TOP/BOTTOM BODY PANELS from light blue felt and sew them together, with the FACE/BACK PANELS, using red thread. The body will be sewn inside out, so remember to have the panel with the mouth and eyes facing inwards. Before sewing up the final panel, leave a small opening to allow the body to be turned the correct way round. Once you've done this, stuff the body with enough toy stuffing to give it a good, sturdy, box shape and then sew up the opening.

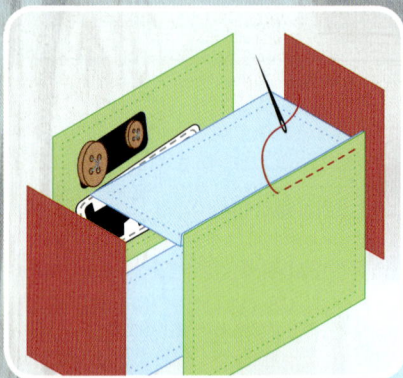

5 Cut one of the HEADPHONE SIDES from black felt and join the two ends together with grey thread. Then cut the HEADPHONE PAD from black felt and sew to the HEADPHONE SIDE.

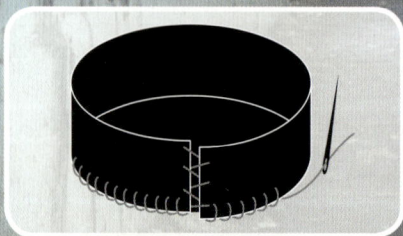

6 Cut one of the HEADPHONE DOMES from patterned fabric and, making sure you have the back of the material facing up, sew together the 'V' with light green thread.

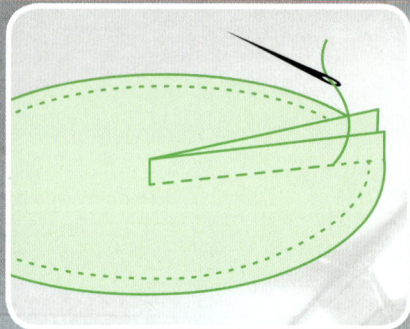

7 Turn the HEADPHONE SIDE/PAD from step 5, inside out. Now sew the HEADPHONE DOME and HEADPHONE SIDE/PAD together with light green thread. Leave a small opening at the end so you can turn the headphone back the correct way. Stuff with a handful of toy stuffing, then sew up the opening.

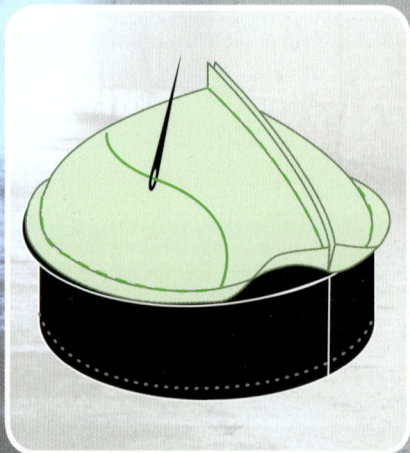

8 Cut the DOME BAND from light blue felt and run a line of overstitches down the two long edges with light blue thread.

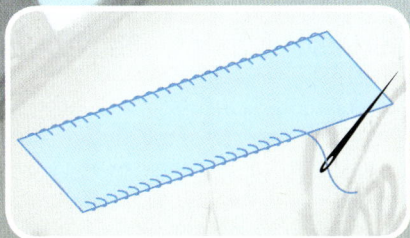

9 Lay the DOME BAND over the HEADPHONE DOME. Make sure the seam on the DOME is facing you and then lay the BAND over the DOME so it crosses the seam. Attach one end of the BAND to the DOME with light blue thread and repeat on the other end of the strap to secure it to the headphone.

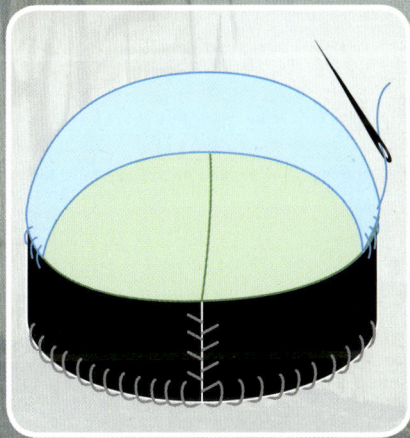

10 Repeat steps 5 to 9 to make the second headphone.

11 Sew the two headphones to the sides of the body with black thread. You only need to attach them at the four corners of the body.

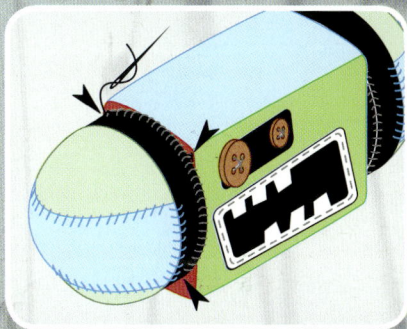

12 Finish by cutting the HEADPHONE STRAP from grey felt and attaching it to each of the headphones with black thread.

Light blue felt, dark blue felt, white felt, light blue fur

Dark blue, white and dark grey embroidery thread

Toy stuffing

Pins, Craft glue

Embroidery needle

Scissors

Templates from page 46

MAKING `MANIC MOUSE`

1 Photocopy or trace all the templates on page 46. Cut the FRONT from light blue felt and then stitch the two open ends together using dark blue thread.

2 Cut the SIDE PANELS from light blue fur and stitch them to the FRONT using dark blue thread.

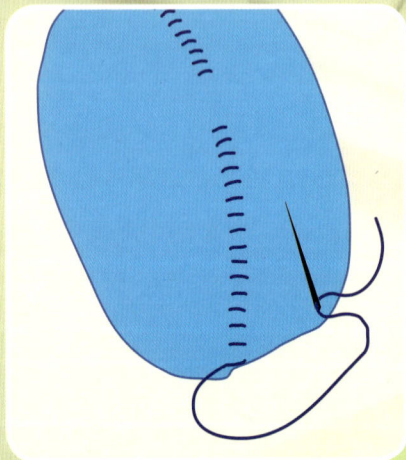

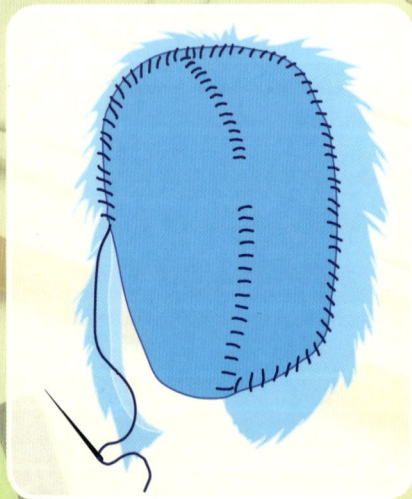

MANIC MOUSE

Ever wanted to learn all of those keyboard shortcuts? This monster is the perfect personal trainer. You'd be angry too if someone was tapping your head every second.

3 Cut the BACK from dark blue felt and stitch it to the SIDE PANELS using white thread. Leave a small opening.

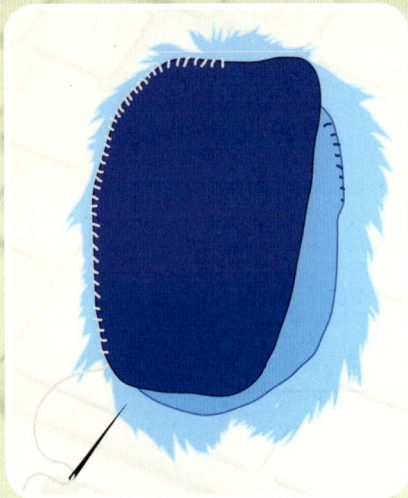

5 Stitch onto the FRONT, to create the mouse button outlines, using dark blue thread.

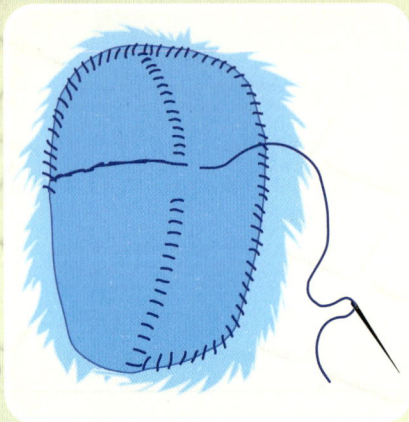

MONSTER MAYHEM!

4 Push the stuffing into the hole and close up the hole with a few stitches in white thread.

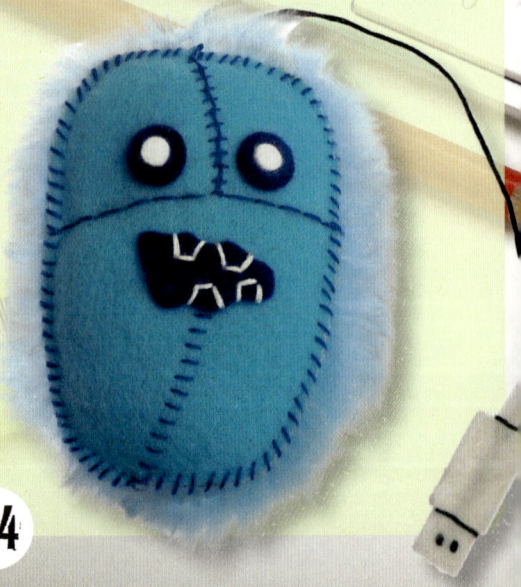

6 Cut out the MOUTH from dark blue felt. Stitch the teeth with white thread and then glue the mouth onto the mouse.

8 Cut out the two USB PLUG pieces from white felt and using a short length of dark grey thread, stitch the detail.

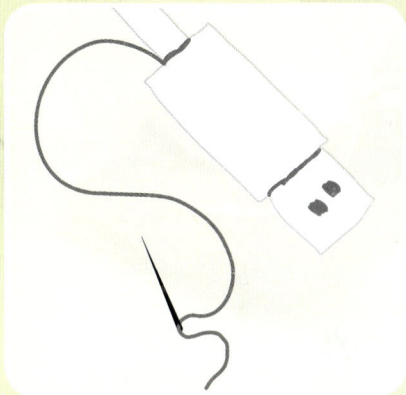

7 Cut out the EYES from dark blue felt and the PUPILS from white felt. Glue them onto the mouse.

9 Cut a 20-cm (8-inch) length of dark grey thread and sew it to the top edge of the mouse. Place the other end of the thread on the back of the USB PLUG. Glue the two USB PLUGS together to sandwich the dark grey thread.

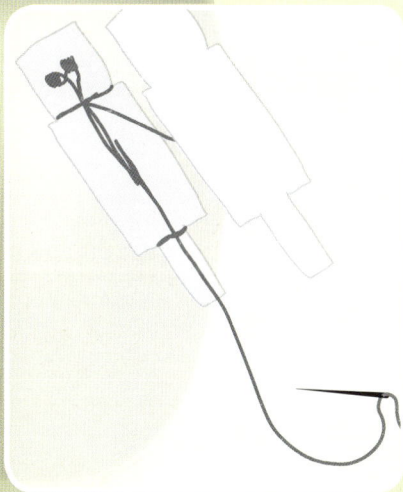

FULL OF BEANS

Highly caffeinated and full of more energy than a Monday morning should ever see. Once unleashed you might regret it.

MAKING `FULL OF BEANS`

1 Photocopy or trace all the templates on page 47. Cut out the CUP and HANDLE from the red felt. Place the HANDLE on one end of the CUP with the HANDLE facing inwards. Curl the CUP over so that the two ends meet, sandwiching the HANDLE between the two ends. Sew down the edge, then turn the whole CUP inside out so that the HANDLE is now on the outside.

2 Cut three 10 x 12-cm (4 x 4¾-inch) pieces of cardboard. Use the double-sided tape to stick the pieces of card on top of each other to make one thick piece. Now cut two 10 x 12-cm (4 x 4¾-inch) pieces of silver fabric and stick them to either side of the card using double-sided tape. Cut this cardboard/fabric sandwich into shape using the SPOON template.

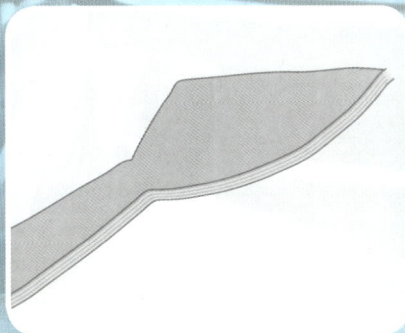

MATERIALS

Red felt, dark brown felt, white felt, light blue felt, silver fabric
Cardboard (from a cereal packet)
White, red, brown and black embroidery thread
2 small black beads
Double-sided tape, Pins, Craft glue
Embroidery needle, Scissors
Templates from page 47

3 Stick a small piece of the double-sided tape to the area shown on the back of the SPOON.

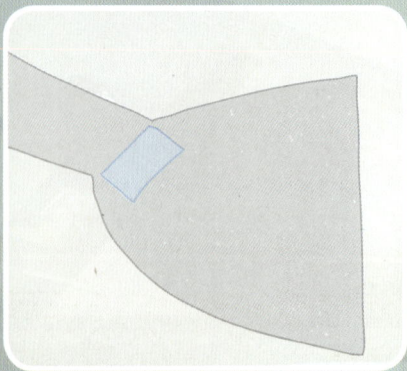

4 Cut the two COFFEE pieces from brown felt. Place the SPOON onto one of the COFFEE pieces and push down to stick.

SMELL THE COFFEE!

5 Sew the two COFFEE pieces together using brown thread, leaving the two semi-circular parts open.

6 Sew the COFFEE to the inside top edge of the CUP (about 8mm/³⁄₈ inch down from the rim) with red thread.

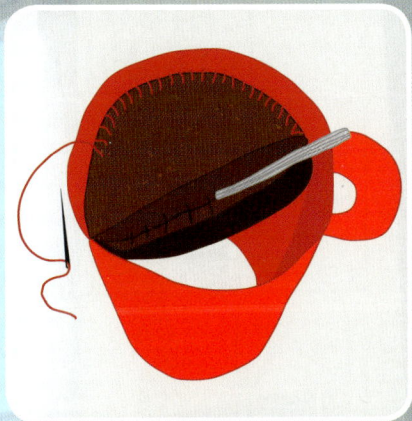

7 Turn the cup upside down. Cut a piece of cardboard about 30cm (12 inches) long and 8cm (3¼ inches) high. Curl the card to form a tube and push into the bottom of the CUP. If any card protrudes from the CUP, trim the card to just below the edge.

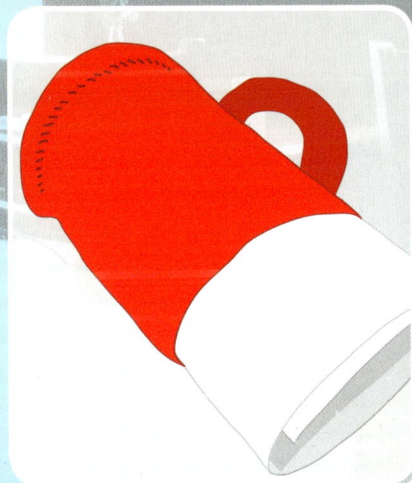

8 Cut out the BASE from red felt and sew it into the bottom of the CUP using white thread.

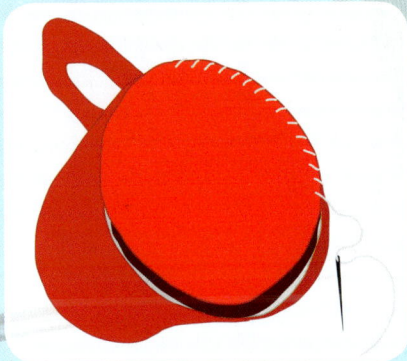

9 Cut out the EYES and MOUTH from white felt and the PUPILS from light blue felt. Sew the PUPIL to the EYE with black thread and a bead to form the centre of the pupil. Finish the monster by gluing the EYES and MOUTH to the COFFEE. Once everything has dried, push the spoon into the cup and the monster's head will disappear. Pull the spoon to free the monster!

FRONT x 2

BACK

CUSHION MONSTER TEMPLATES

MOUTH x 2

NAIL

BONE

FINGER x 2

DOTS x 27

DIZZY DIE
TEMPLATES

INSIDE x 2

BODY

EYE

SIDE x 4

EYE

TOOTH

GUTSY TEMPLATES

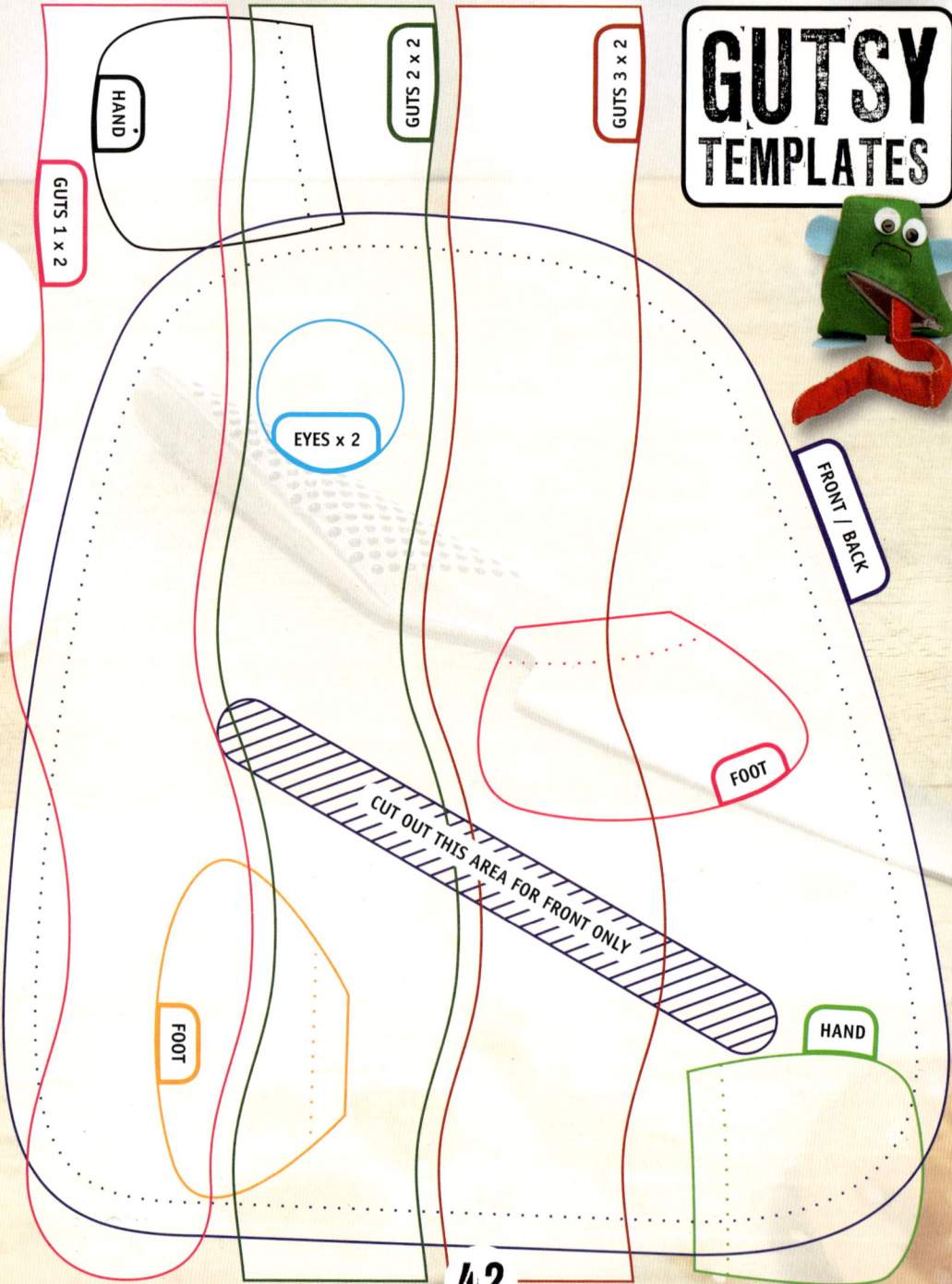

HAND

GUTS 1 x 2

GUTS 2 x 2

GUTS 3 x 2

EYES x 2

FRONT / BACK

FOOT

CUT OUT THIS AREA FOR FRONT ONLY

FOOT

HAND

42

SOCK MONSTER TEMPLATES

BACK PANEL

DOOR

CUT OUT THIS AREA

FRONT PANEL

SIDE PANELS x 2

SOCKS x 2

EYE

TEETH

CUT OUT THIS AREA

END PANELS x 2

EYE

MOUTH x 2

WEBSTER TEMPLATES

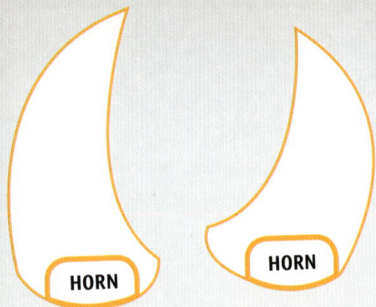

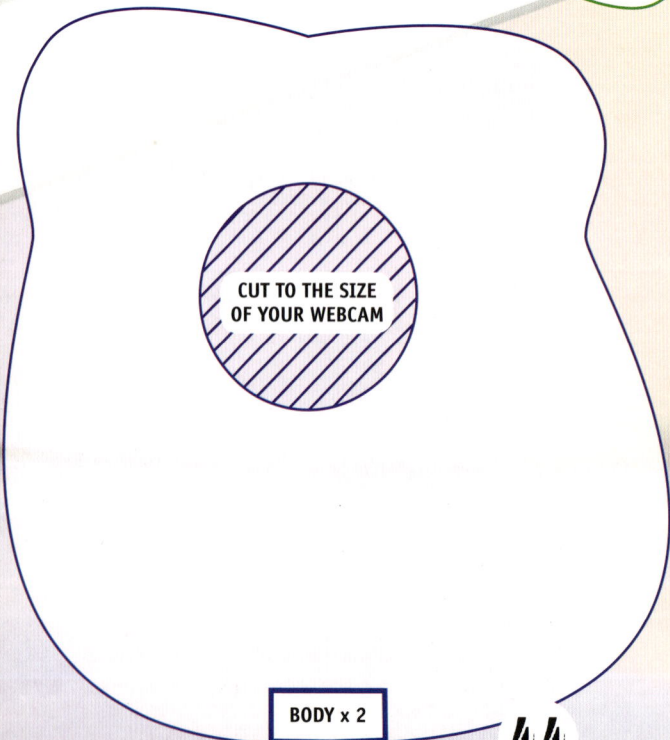

HORN

HORN

EYELASHES

RIGHT ARM

LEFT ARM

PAW AND CLAWS x 2

CUT TO THE SIZE OF YOUR WEBCAM

TOOTH

TOOTH

BODY x 2

DOME BAND x 2

HEADPHONE STRAP

PLAY IT LOUD! TEMPLATES

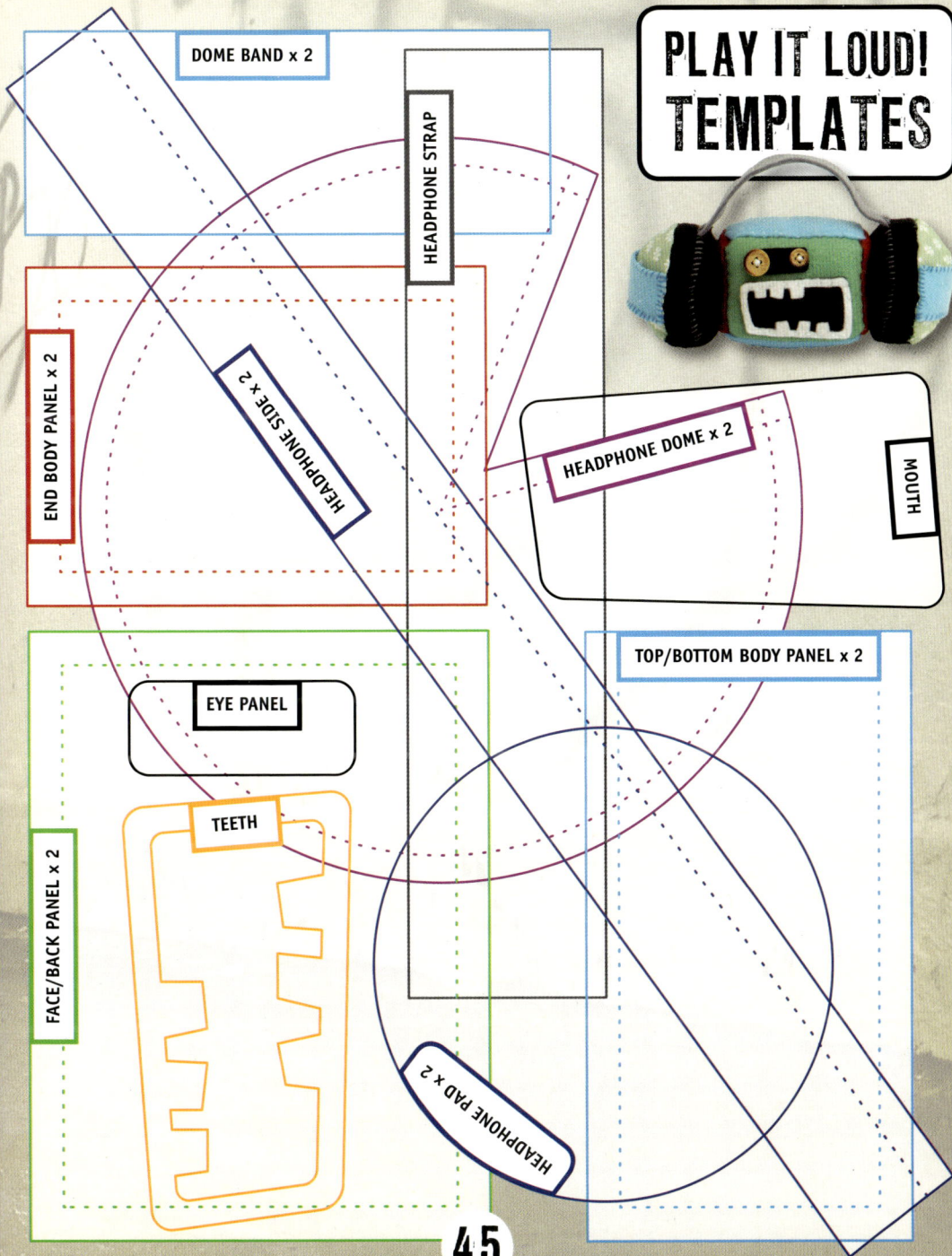

END BODY PANEL x 2

HEADPHONE SIDE x 2

HEADPHONE DOME x 2

MOUTH

EYE PANEL

TOP/BOTTOM BODY PANEL x 2

TEETH

FACE/BACK PANEL x 2

HEADPHONE PAD x 2

MANIC MOUSE TEMPLATES

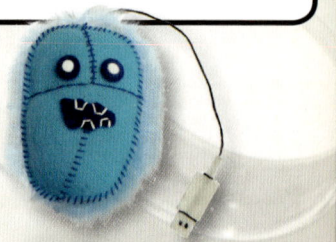

FRONT

SIDE PANELS x 2

EYES x 2

PUPILS X 2

BACK

MOUTH

USB PLUG x 2

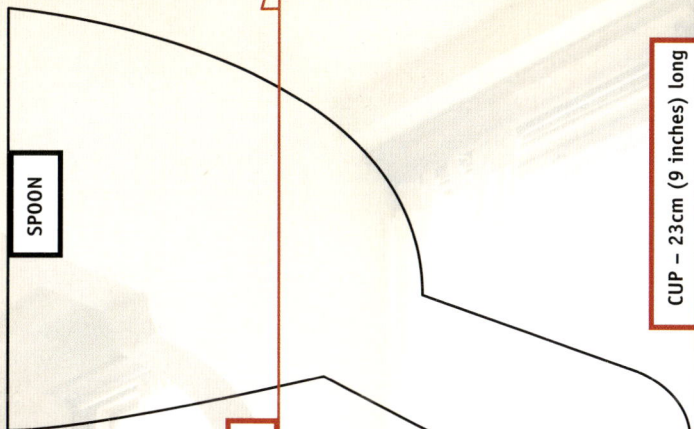

SPOON

CUP – 23cm (9 inches) long

CUP – 23cm (9 inches) long

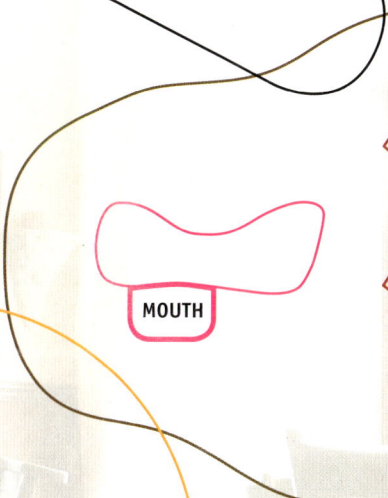

MOUTH

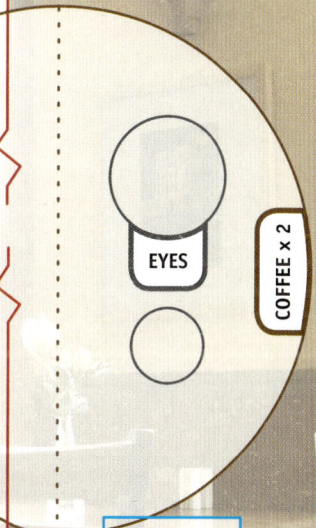

PUPILS X 2

EYES

COFFEE x 2

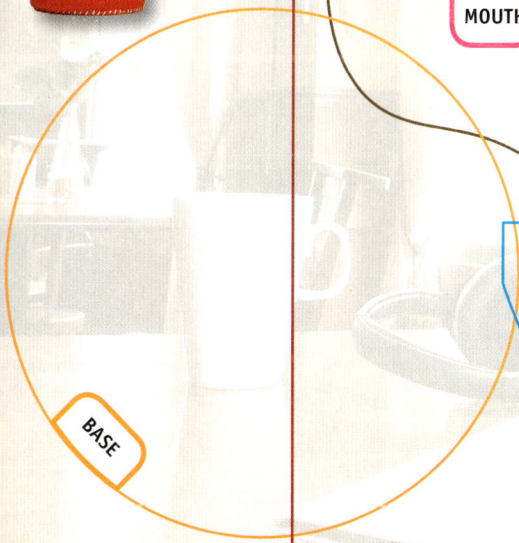

BASE

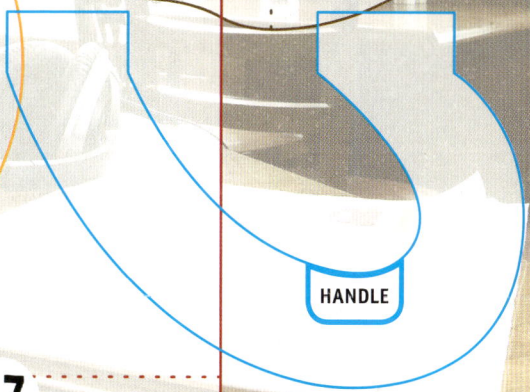

HANDLE

A
arms 26, 44

B
beans, coffee *see* Full of Beans
bones, finger 11, 40
buttons 11, 14, 18, 22, 29

C
claws 26, 44
coffee 38, 39, 47
    see also Full of Beans
computer mouse 32–35, 46
cup, coffee 37, 39, 47
Cushion Monster 8–11
    materials 8
    templates 8, 40

D
die 12–15, 41
Dizzy Die 12–15
    materials 13
    templates 13, 41

E
eyes 11, 15, 18, 22, 26, 29, 30,
    35, 39, 41, 42, 43, 45, 46, 47
    eyelashes 26, 44

F
feet 16, 42
fingers 11, 40
    fingernails 11, 40
Full of Beans 36–39
    materials 37
    templates 37, 47

G
gluing 11, 15, 18, 24, 26, 29, 35
guts 17, 18, 19, 42
Gutsy 16–19
    materials 16
    templates 16, 42

H
hands 16, 42
headphones 30, 45
horns 26, 44

M
Manic Mouse 32–35
    materials 32
    templates 32, 46
materials
    Cushion Monster 8
    Dizzy Die 13
    Full of Beans 37
    Gutsy 16
    Manic Mouse 32
    Play it Loud! 29
    Sock Monster 20
    Webster the Webcam
        Monster 24
mouse, computer 32–35, 46
mouth parts 10, 15, 18, 21, 23,
    24, 29, 30, 35, 39, 40, 43, 45,
    46, 47

P
paws 26, 44
Play it Loud! 28–31
    materials 29
    templates 29, 45

R
radio *see* Play it Loud!

S
sewing 8, 10, 11, 13, 14, 18, 19,
    21, 22, 23, 27, 29, 30, 31, 35,
    38, 39
    see also stitching
Sock Monster 20–23
    materials 21
    templates 21, 43
socks 23, 43
spoon, coffee 37, 38
stitching 14, 15, 16, 18, 24, 26,
    29, 32, 34, 35
    see also sewing
stuffing 11, 13, 18, 23, 26, 30,
    34

T
teeth 15, 22, 24, 29, 35, 41, 43,
    44, 45
templates
    Cushion Monster 40
    Dizzy Die 41
    Full of Beans 47
    Gutsy 42
    Manic Mouse 46
    Play it Loud! 45
    Sock Monster 43
    Webster the Webcam
        Monster 44

U
USB plugs 35, 46

W
webcam 24–27, 44
Webster the Webcam Monster
    24–27
    materials 24
    templates 24, 44

Z
zips 8, 16